To

♥

*Loving
Relationships*

Ten Keys to Loving Relationships

GUDRUN KRETSCHMANN

Thorsons
An Imprint of HarperCollins*Publishers*

Thorsons
An Imprint of HarperCollins *Publishers*
77-85 Fulham Palace Road,
Hammersmith, London W6 8JB

First published in Australia by Angus&Robertson,
25 Ryde Road, Pymble, Sydney, NSW 2073, 1994
Thorsons edition 1994
1 3 5 7 9 10 8 6 4 2

© Gudrun Kretschmann 1994
Illustrations by Kate Mitchell

Gudrun Kretschmann asserts the moral right to
be identified as the author of this work

A catalogue record for this book
is available from the British Library

ISBN 0 7225 3004 8
Printed in Hong Kong

All rights reserved. No part of this publication may be reproduced,
stored in a retrieval system, or transmitted, in any form or by any
means, electronic, mechanical, photocopying, recording or
otherwise, without the prior permission of the publishers.

Dear Friends

This book is about creating and having a loving relationship. What does a loving relationship mean to you? We all have different ideas about this. Remember we are in relationship with everyone and everything around us. But let's presume that we are talking about the relationship with the one person who we feel differently about, who we want to share a lot of time and intimate moments with and who seems most important to us.

Loving relationships are never-ending lessons and these keys will help you towards manifesting a relationship you deserve and desire.

Love

Gudrun

Contents

Creation
Commitment
Truth
Responsibility
Personal growth
Acceptance
Giving
Self-love
Creativity
Intimacy

1

Creation

TEN KEYS TO LOVING RELATIONSHIPS

I need to feel self-love first, before I am able to love someone else.

It is important to feel your self-love before you are able to love someone else. Be clear about what you want in a partner. Make a list of all the qualities you would like in him/her. Then start developing these qualities in yourself. Act as if you already have someone in your life who you love dearly and who loves you with the same sincerity. Get the feeling for what it is like to love and to be loved. Breathe it in and believe you are worthy of it. There is no need to search for your soul mate. Searching stops you from forming other relationships and friendships along the way. You are not able to control when and where you will meet your ideal partner. Start to treat yourself the way you would like your partner to treat you. Be pleased with yourself at all times; dress nicely, buy yourself flowers, enjoy your work. Surrender to what happens and give up forcing things. Meeting your perfect partner will happen at the right time, when you least expect it, and maybe a relationship will develop with the person you least expect. Enjoy yourself with those you are with. Enjoy life now.

2

Commitment

TEN KEYS TO LOVING RELATIONSHIPS

I am with my partner 100% or not at all

Commitment means love; the essence of every relationship, whatever form it takes. Without commitment there is no loving relationship. Commitment solves problems, brings happiness and strengthens the connection between you and your partner. It also means freedom. Many of us see a committed relationship as a jail believing that we cannot do what we want to do. The thought of 'the grass might be greener on the other side' keeps us from being passionate and truly enjoying a relationship in which we can grow together, learn from each other and feel a deep connection. Stay in the present.

It does not matter whether you will be together for the rest of your lives or not, but the desire to do so means commitment. Be with your partner 100% or not at all. Be clear about what kind of relationship you want and with whom. We often compromise ourselves to the point of risking our health. Listen to your heart. It will give you the right answer. Be committed to yourself; to love and honour your own being. Trust yourself and go with the flow.

3

Truth

TEN KEYS TO LOVING RELATIONSHIPS

I create harmony by seeking and speaking the truth fast

TEN KEYS TO LOVING RELATIONSHIPS

Truth expressed immediately is the foundation a loving relationship can build on. A satisfactory relationship will not survive if true feelings, thoughts and actions are being withheld. Be open with your partner. Communicate your feelings and thoughts. We only communicate 7% verbally. If you don't speak the truth quickly it just complicates and prolongs, but truth will find its way to the surface somehow. Truth is an attribute of love. Love is not complete without truth. There is an old belief that truth hurts. The truth is you can never hurt another person with the words you speak! The other person is totally responsible for his/her reactions and feelings. However, there are kind and unkind, appropriate and inappropriate ways of telling the truth. Make an I-Statement. Say, 'I feel angry that you didn't do the washing-up as promised' and not, 'You make me angry . . .' Your partner may not be able to pick up on your body language or the look in your eyes and vice versa. Never presume that you know what your partner feels if it hasn't been communicated. Your own perception often distorts the picture. Use your intuition and avoid misunderstandings, confusion and arguments by speaking and seeking the truth. Be true to yourself. Ask for what you want. Guilt and fear will drop away once you deal with them straightaway. Trust yourself.

4

Responsibility

TEN KEYS TO LOVING RELATIONSHIPS

I never think I am the victim.

We are responsible for what is happening to us. Situations and circumstances are consciously or subconsciously chosen and created by us. We attract the right people to learn our lessons with and to recognise our own choices. We are not the victim of someone else's actions but of our own thoughts. If there are arguments and conflict in your relationship ask yourself, 'Why is this happening? What is it in me that creates this situation?' Do not blame or judge your partner. Take responsibility for what is happening or what you perceive is happening to you. What we see, like or dislike in others, we see, like or dislike in ourselves. We need to look at ourselves first. Trying to change our partner does not succeed. Accept that he/she is different. If we want change, we need to change first. Find out where your own and your partner's boundaries are and make sure they are communicated.

Discover your own patterns and dependencies. There is a lot of manipulation in relationships because of the fear of losing out. Don't take comments and behaviour personally.

Your partner's actions may trigger thoughts and feelings in you but it is your choice to act or react. When he/she is angry, recognise that something triggered these feelings that may not have anything to do with you. Communication is vital.

5

Personal Growth

TEN KEYS TO LOVING RELATIONSHIPS

*Personal growth unites people
and opens many doors.*

Making the commitment to grow as an individual and to learn more about ourselves will help us recognise, accept and love each other. Learn about relationships and co-dependence. All of us have to learn to relate to each other, especially on a more intimate and deeper level. Grow spiritually and support each other in areas you feel need improvement. Create safety in your relationship so that so-called 'negative' feelings can be accepted and dealt with. Heal your childhood and reclaim your inner child with the support of your partner. Listen to each other. Committing yourselves to growing personally together will deepen the connection. It unites people and opens doors that would have stayed closed if you had tried it on your own. Be committed to overcoming any hurdles along the way and fulfilling excitement will be the reward. Often the path towards this goal brings lessons which will help you move beyond your limitations. If you are true to yourself the relationship will reveal itself in a unique and fascinating way. Go with the flow. You will recognise this to be an everlasting but exciting journey.

6

Acceptance

TEN KEYS TO LOVING RELATIONSHIPS

Happiness does not depend on anybody or anything else but me.

What would happen if we totally accepted ourselves, our looks, our age, our body, our qualities, our faults and our feelings? Would it still matter if the one we love paid more attention to someone else? Acceptance of self is acceptance of others. Allow your partner to be who and what he/she is. There is no need to 'fix' the other person by trying to make them the way we want them to be. We all do the best we know how at the time. Forgiveness is the key to peace and harmony. Happiness does not depend on the behaviour of another person. Let's take responsibility and recognise our part in the game. Then jealousy, which is a feeling or thought of inferiority or the fear of loss, cannot exist, as we are already complete. It will be difficult for us to see anyone or anything as a threat, because self-acceptance cannot be threatened nor destroyed, unless we allow it. Many of our behaviour patterns and feelings have origins in childhood, when we experienced separation or a fear of abandonment. We often act out of fear until we accept and acknowledge our feelings and realise that love is unlimited and cannot be taken away or divided. There is enough love for everyone.

7

Giving

TEN KEYS TO LOVING RELATIONSHIPS

Giving and expecting something in return is conditional and does not really mean giving.

Do you love and believe in your partner? Do you give him/her your full support? Honest constructive feedback, not criticism, expressing compliments and appreciation, are vital in a loving relationship. Never take your partner for granted. Treat your partner the way you want to be treated. Let him/her know that you are happy in their company. There are many ways of doing so: verbal statements, giving little presents (not just on birthdays and anniversaries), creating surprises, or supporting your partner emotionally. Let your partner know that you are privileged to be in a relationship with him/her. Giving and expecting something in return is conditional and does not really mean giving. Give from your heart, enjoy the giving, then it will be receiving at the same time. However, giving can be one-sided in relationships. It may be a sign of co-dependence, meaning that we subconsciously depend on the reaction of our partner. Create a healthy balance.

8

Self-love

TEN KEYS TO LOVING RELATIONSHIPS

What I see in others, I see in myself

Love yourself and your body. Be beautiful and attractive. Look after yourself. Dress nicely and smell good (even after 20 years of marriage). Be beautiful for yourself at any time, whether you are with someone or not, whether you are on holiday or at work, whether you are a man or a woman. Be in love with yourself without arrogance. Take time out just for yourself. Do whatever you love doing without guilt. Exercise, meditate, take a bath with incense and candlelight, go for early morning walks on the beach. Realise how beautiful you are, whether your partner tells you so or

not. Don't depend on compliments. They are not necessary if you know yourself. Feel your strength and greatness when alone. Be independent. Independence does not mean loneliness or separation.
It leads to self-acceptance and realisation of our own capabilities. Standing on our own feet emotionally and financially is a great bonus in any relationship. Seeing the beauty in ourselves will enable us to see it in others. Through accepting our greatness we accept the greatness in others.

9

Creativity

*Routine can bring comfort
but also boredom*

Changes bring life and creativity into our relationships. If a certain routine has settled in which brings comfort but boredom, create change. If you have been doing something a certain way for a long time because it suits you, try doing it differently for a change. You can always change back if you want to. Be spontaneous, have fun, make fun, especially if everything seems a bit too serious and heavy. Do something together that brings out excitement and the giggle in you. Take time out, play, be children. Not enough money or time, or the children, etc, are just good excuses to stay in your

comfort zone, but there are no hurdles that cannot be overcome. Give each other enough space and develop your own interests and hobbies if you have been doing everything together so far. Create togetherness and common goals if you have been doing everything separately. Create balance in any area where there is a surplus or lack.
Be creative.

10

Intimacy

My body tells me the truth

When we begin to be intimate in a relationship we step over boundaries and become more vulnerable to the other person, and vice versa. It gives us the opportunity to get to know each other on a deeper, different level. It shows us sides of the person we have not seen before. Childhood memories or emotional stress are often buried behind bedroom walls. Listen to your body. How does it feel when touching, stroking, hugging or making love? Recognising our body signs will take us closer to our own truth. Our bodies are messengers of our inner being. Do what feels right and not what you think is right. Follow your feelings and share them with your partner even though it may be a little frightening to do so. To experience intimacy be 100% present, be open and tell the truth, take responsibility if you are not happy, work through problems together without blame, accept your differences, make them attractive and versatile and create fun. Let go of guilt and all programmed thoughts about intimacy. Sometimes it may feel right just to lie together or massage each other. Allow yourself to experience the beauty and harmony of making love.